the nobody

leanne m.

BookLeaf Publishing

India | USA | UK

Presentation by *BookLeaf Publishing*

Web: www.bookleafpub.com

E-mail: info@bookleafpub.com

ISBN: 9789363304963

First edition 2024

the mirror

every day you open your eyes
walk to the mirror
and stare back.

"i am still not good enough", you say
you say through tears
and screams
and endless regret.

they don't get it.
no one does.
you was born you and
they were born
lucky.

they're gifted
they're pretty
they're smart
they're
everything
to someone.

you're
nothing
to

everyone.

-the nobody

i'm sorry

sorry you say for
every
single
thing
sorry you say
even when they
trample.
crumple.
destroy.
your own heart.

they twist
they shove
the push you so far
so deep
so excruciatingly deep
that every motion
every breath
feels like glass shards
in your lungs.

pain so vulgar that
even a nobody
could feel you.

-the nobody

400 pound girl

i never look the same.
one day
i'm a 400 pound girl
and the next
i'm 150

the scale says 105
but it's lying, i know.
it's lying
it's lying lying lying
just like my
f r i e n d s

the ones who say
"you're pretty"
then snicker.
they don't even wait
for me
to walk
away.

they want you to cry
they want you to feel
so small
that once again

you're nothing at all.

you pinch your cheek,
look at your thighs,
look at your stomach,
and look away.
you fear for tomorrow
just like
you feared for
today.

-the nobody

i'm no one

why do fears carve out your heart
so much
that all is left
is nothing at all

you become no one
no name
no feelings
no identity
just a hallow vessel
vying to be seen

everything is swirling
your heart
threatens
to leap out

your lip is quavering
knees are shaking
hands are falling apart
from the endless punches
thrown at your poor wall

why do i still
feel

like
someone

i know
i'm
no.
one.

just another nod in the hallway
just another forced smile
but not even that.
they don't even see you.

-the nobody

behind

i'm always left behind
on the sidewalk

somehow
someway
even if everyone is there
i end up alone

i'm always five steps behind
five jokes behind
five hangouts behind

we must've told you,
they say
if they must've told me
then i must be zendaya

this guy "liked" me somehow.
he touched me.
kissed me.

but he dated other girls too
without telling me.
and
everyone.

knew.

how funny
i must've been behind on that too.

-the nobody

glitter

you trust.
mistake.
you confide.
mistake.

secrets secrets secrets
how dangerous
in the
wrong
hands

they always end up in the wrong hands
but who's fault is that?
mine.

secrets fall like glitter
impossible to stop
impossible to clean up
impossible.

-the nobody

glances

they look at you
differently.
it's something in their eyes
something in their glance
their tone

it's not pity.
but it is.
it's not horror.
but it is.

talk to someone,
they say
you're not okay,
they say
you're doing this to yourself
by not asking for help,
they say

how can they say that
to me.
how.
can.
they.

i'm drowning.
i'm literally drowning.

i'm sorry
i said anything
at all.

-the nobody

i'm not there

i'm not there
once
again

i'm not there
where the laughter
echoes
off walls

i'm not there
where happiness
beams
like sunshine

i'm not there
where people share
warm embraces

i
a shadow
in daylight
a whisper lost
among the stars

i

a muted song
a letter that was
never
opened

i
a mess
who's hands
only find
air.

i'm not there.

-the nobody

puzzle piece

i am a puzzle piece
trying to fit
where i am
not
needed.

i try
and i try
and i try
and i try
and why is that
not good enough

not good enough should be my name
not good enough is written all over me

i'm not good enough to be remembered
i'm not good enough to be a nobody

because at least a nobody
would still fit
in the puzzle

a nobody could be a part of the moon
or a tree

or the corner of an ice cream

my piece doesn't exist
my piece is an error.
an extra.
a mistake.

-the nobody

anger

anger is like a novel.
it doesn't seep out
until the chapters build up
up.
up.

the climax, well

the climax is when
you
snap.

some things you can't talk about
you just. can't.
even though it wasn't your fault
even though you were hurt

the shame.
the sadness.
the feeling of no control.

it's just
overwhelming
it just
builds

up

it makes
even breathing
feel like you are stuck in your own skin

i am itching to be free.
please.

i am tired of all the drama
and trauma
and working all day
just to end up coming to an atmosphere
where yelling is okay

i am angry
that people
can even be this way.

-the nobody

healing

healing feels like
breaking yourself apart
again
and building yourself back up
from nothing.

healing is full of pain
and struggle
and the only thing keeping you going
is misguided hope
that one day
things will become less gray

-the nobody

sand

it's like i'm
trying to build a castle
in
s h i f t i n g
sand.

-the nobody

tears

fire. heat.
blistering waves of desolation.
all out. all gone.
tears.

a passion snuffed out.
so fast. so swift.
words cut like a knife.
tears.

a touch. a kiss.
a mistake.
a violation.
tears.

no longer somebody.
just an object
no longer of use.
tears.

-the nobody

honey

honey drips
from lips,
sweet syrup
spills,

words that coat
like sugar
on a lie.

they catch flies with honey,
not vinegar.

i'm blinded by gloss
the trap
hidden
by golden sheen.

lies
d i s s o l v e
like honey in tea.
tea that burns the throat
though iced.

-the nobody

shadows

my mind is
filled with
shadows.
they
twist.
turn.
break.

but unlike me
these shadows
are
somebody.

they're clawing
and clawing
and clawing away
until
my sanity is broken.
not only a nobody
but a lunatic now too.

half-lit.
half lost.
stuck.
light no longer pulls.

just shadow.

-the nobody

cracking

words are like feathers.
light.
soft.
but even feathers can
turn to
stone.

"words can't hurt," they say.
"just ignore them," they say.

but they push.
and they push.
and they push.

the wall is cracking.
cracking.

the pieces
that used to believe
in humanity
have fallen.

-the nobody

camera

lights.
camera.
action.

smile!
pretend nothing happened!
smile!

sweat.
fear.
done.

-the nobody

dreams

fireflies dancing
in jars
of hope.
glowing.
beaming.

but
time
is a
thief.
a cloak
of
darkness.

it stole
the light
the dreams
the future

it stole
my life
from me.

-the nobody